COLLEGE
BASKETBALL'S
CHAMPIONSHIP

BY TYLER OMOTH

CAPSTONE PRESS
a capstone imprint

Blazers Books are published by Capstone Press,
1710 Roe Crest Drive, North Mankato, Minnesota 56003
www.mycapstone.com

Library of Congress Cataloging-in-Publication Data
Names: Omoth, Tyler, author.
Title: College basketball's championship / By Tyler Omoth.
Description: North Mankato, Minnesota : Capstone Press, [2018] | Series:
    Major sports championships. | Audience: Age 8-14.
Identifiers: LCCN 2017028551 (print) | LCCN 2017032371 (ebook) | ISBN
    9781543504750 (eBook PDF) | ISBN 9781543504958 (hardcover)
Subjects: LCSH: NCAA Basketball Tournament—History—Juvenile literature. |
    Basketball—Tournaments—United States—History—Juvenile literature.
    Sports—Equipment and supplies—Juvenile literature.
Classification: LCC GV885.49.N37 (ebook) | LCC GV885.49.N37 O46 2018 (print)
    |DDC 796.323/63—dc23
LC record available at https://lccn.loc.gov/2017028551

Editorial Credits
Carrie Braulick Sheely, editor; Kyle Grenz, designer; Eric Gohl, media researcher;
Kathy McColley, production specialist

Photo Credits
Getty Images: Bettmann, 17, Carl Skalak, 24, David E. Klutho, 27, Drew Angerer, 13,
James Drake, 18–19, NCAA Photos, 9; Newscom: Icon Sportswire DBA/Leslie Plaza
Johnson, 20, UPI/Gary C. Caskey, 7, USA Today Sports/Bob Donnan, cover, 15, USA
Today Sports/Reuters, 10–11, USA Today Sports/Robert Deutsch, 5, ZUMA Press/
Minneapolis Star Tribune, 23, ZUMA Press/Pool/Chris Steppig, 28

Design Elements: Shutterstock

Printed and bound in the USA.
010754S18

TABLE OF CONTENTS

A BREATHTAKING BUZZER BEATER

The 2016 **NCAA** men's basketball championship game was a thriller. North Carolina's Marcus Paige tied the game with just seconds left. Then Villanova's Kris Jenkins shot a long three-pointer as the buzzer blared. Swish! Villanova won!

FACT The most famous TV voice and face of the men's **Final Four** is Dick Vitale. Vitale's lively comments have been part of the Final Four since 1979.

NCAA—stands for the National Collegiate Athletic Association; the NCAA makes rules for college sports in the United States

Final Four—the final four teams of the yearly NCAA basketball championships; each team is a regional winner

Kris Jenkins shoots a buzzer beater to win the 2016 NCAA men's basketball championship.

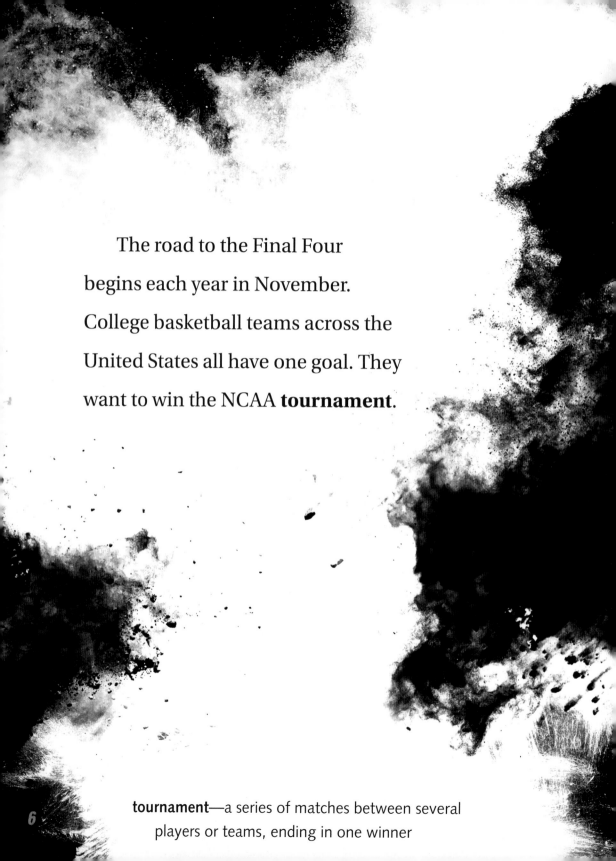

The road to the Final Four begins each year in November. College basketball teams across the United States all have one goal. They want to win the NCAA **tournament**.

tournament—a series of matches between several players or teams, ending in one winner

In 1982 broadcaster Brent Musberger called the NCAA tournament "March Madness." The nickname stuck.

HISTORY OF THE CHAMPIONSHIP

In 1939 eight teams played in the first NCAA basketball tournament. The University of Oregon faced off against Ohio State in the championship game. Oregon won the title. About 5,000 fans watched the game.

Ohio State's John Schick makes a basket during the first NCAA championship game in 1939.

FACT Ohio State's Jimmy Hull was named the Most Outstanding Player of the 1939 tournament. He scored 58 points in three games.

The number of teams and fans has grown over the years. Today 68 teams play in the tournament. In 2017 more than 76,000 fans cheered on their favorite team in the championship game.

FACT The 2017 NCAA tournament averaged 9.8 million TV viewers for each regular game. The regional finals averaged 10.2 million viewers.

In the 2017 men's NCAA championship game, the North Carolina Tar Heels defeated the Gonzaga Bulldogs.

THE ROAD TO THE FINAL FOUR

Every year in March, a committee chooses 68 teams to compete in the NCAA tournament. A computer **ranking** system helps rank the teams. The teams are placed in a tournament **bracket**. The top four teams get a number-one **seed**.

rank—to assign a position to

bracket—a way to organize teams in a tournament

seed—a team's ranking in the NCAA basketball tournament, based on the team's region and conference

The 2017 tournament selection committee meets in New York City to begin making team selections.

The tournament breaks teams into four groups called regions. If a team loses, it is out of the tournament. When only four teams are left, it is called the Final Four. Finally, two teams are left. They face off in the championship game.

MOST TEAM FINAL FOUR APPEARANCES

TEAM	APPEARANCES
NORTH CAROLINA	20
UCLA	17
KENTUCKY	17
DUKE	16
KANSAS	14

Gonzaga's Jordan Mathews defends North Carolina's forward Justin Jackson in the 2017 NCAA men's championship game.

GREATEST TEAM DYNASTIES

Some teams make winning look easy. University of California-Los Angeles (UCLA) won 10 NCAA titles from 1964 to 1975. Coach John Wooden's **dynasty** also had four undefeated seasons during this time.

FACT From 1967 to 1973, UCLA won seven straight titles.

dynasty—a team that wins multiple championships over a period of several years

The UCLA players celebrate after winning the championship title against Dayton in 1967.

MOST TEAM CHAMPIONSHIP WINS

TEAM	WINS	YEARS
UCLA	11	1964, 1965, 1967, 1968, 1969, 1970, 1971, 1972, 1973, 1975, 1995
KENTUCKY	8	1948, 1949, 1951, 1958, 1978, 1996, 1998, 2012
N.C.	6	1957, 1982, 1993, 2005, 2009, 2017
DUKE	5	1991, 1992, 2001, 2010, 2015

After Wooden retired, the Indiana Hoosiers became the team to beat. From 1971 to 2000, coach Bobby Knight led the Hoosiers to the Final Four five times. The team brought home three titles.

FACT In 1975-76, the Hoosiers went 32-0. No other men's NCAA basketball team has had a **perfect season** since.

perfect season—a sports season in which a team remains undefeated for the regular season and for the playoffs

The Indiana Hoosiers became the NCAA men's basketball champions after beating Michigan in 1976.

Duke's coach Mike Krzyzewski cuts down the net after winning the championship in 2015.

FACT In 1947 North Carolina State won a conference title. Head coach Everett Case cut down the net as a **souvenir**. Ever since, cutting down the net has been a tradition for the NCAA champion.

souvenir—an object kept as a reminder of a person, place, or event

Mike Krzyzewski began coaching Duke in 1980. In 2011 he became the most winning coach in NCAA history. The Blue Devils and "Coach K" have won five titles in 12 Final Four trips.

MOST CHAMPIONSHIP WINS BY COACH

COACH	TEAM	WINS	YEARS
JOHN WOODEN	UCLA	10	1964, 1965, 1967, 1968, 1969, 1970, 1971, 1972, 1973, 1975
MIKE KRZYZEWSKI	DUKE	5	1991, 1992, 2001, 2010, 2015
ADOLPH RUPP	KENTUCKY	4	1948, 1949, 1951, 1958
BOBBY KNIGHT	INDIANA	3	1976, 1981, 1987
JIM CALHOUN	CONNECTICUT	3	1999, 2004, 2011

MEMORABLE MOMENTS

In the 1983 championship game, **underdog** North Carolina State (NC State) was tied with Houston. NC State's Dereck Whittenburg launched a long shot. But it was too short. Teammate Lorenzo Charles dunked it through the hoop for the win.

FACT Not even the top-seeded teams are safe from **upsets.** But a number-sixteen seed team has never beaten a number-one seed team.

underdog—a person or team that is not expected to win an event

upset—a win by a team that was expected to lose

Lorenzo Charles dunks the game-winning basket against Houston in the 1983 championship game.

Villanova's Harold Pressley (right of ball) tries for a score in the 1985 championship game.

In 1985 the Villanova Wildcats were a number-eight seed. The Georgetown Hoyas were a number-one seed and the current champs. The teams met in the championship game. Villanova pulled off the win 66-64. They became the lowest seed to ever win the title.

MOST POINTS SCORED IN A SINGLE TOURNAMENT

POINTS	NAME	SCHOOL	YEAR	TOTAL GAMES PLAYED
184	GLEN RICE	MICHIGAN	1989	6
177	BILL BRADLEY	PRINCETON	1965	5
167	ELVIN HAYES	HOUSTON	1968	5
163	DANNY MANNING	KANSAS	1988	6

FACT Villanova shot an amazing 78 percent in the 1985 championship game.

In the 1993 championship game, Michigan trailed North Carolina by two points. The last 20 seconds ticked down. Michigan's Chris Webber called a timeout. But Michigan didn't have any timeouts left! The mistake cost Michigan a **technical foul** and the ball. North Carolina won.

FACT North Carolina and Kansas played in the longest championship game in 1957. It took three overtime periods before North Carolina won 54-53.

technical foul—a foul that does not involve physical contact between opposing players

Chris Webber calls the fateful timeout that cost his team the championship.

In 2015 the championship game was a battle of number-one seeds. Wisconsin played Duke in a fight to the finish. The lead changed 13 times in the first half alone. Near the end, Wisconsin was ahead by 9 points. But with an exciting **rally**, Duke took the win.

Duke's Justise Winslow fights for a shot between two defenders in the 2015 championship game.

rally—to come from behind to tie or take the lead

Glossary

bracket (BRAK-it)—a way to organize teams in a tournament; as teams win they advance through the bracket to the championship game

conference (KON-fur-uhnss)—a group of athletic teams

dynasty (DYE-nuh-stee)—a team that wins multiple championships over a period of several years

Final Four (FYE-nuhl FOR)—the final four teams of the yearly NCAA basketball championships; each team is the winner of its regional tournament

NCAA—stands for the National Collegiate Athletic Association; the NCAA makes rules for college sports in the United States

perfect season (PUR-fict SEE-zuhn)—a sports season in which a team remains undefeated for the regular season and for the playoffs

rally (RAL-ee)—to come from behind to tie or take the lead

rank (RANGK)—to assign a position to

seed (SEED)—a team's ranking in the NCAA tournament, based on the team's region and conference

souvenir (soo-vuh-NIHR)—an object kept as a reminder of a person, place, or event

technical foul (TEK-ni-kuhl FOUL)—a foul that does not involve physical contact between opposing players

three-pointer (THREE POINT-ur)—a basketball shot or field goal from beyond the three-point line

tournament (TUR-nuh-muhnt)—a series of games between several teams, ending in one winner

underdog (UN-duhr-dawg)—a person or team that is not expected to win an event

upset (UHP-set)—a win by a team that was expected to lose

Read More

Doeden, Matt. *All About Basketball.* All About Sports. North Mankato, Minn.: Capstone, 2015.

Nelson, Robin. *Basketball is Fun!* Sports Are Fun! Minneapolis: Lerner, 2014.

Storden, Thom. *Amazing Basketball Records.* Epic Sports Records. North Mankato, Minn.: Capstone, 2015.

Internet Sites

Use FactHound to find Internet sites related to this book.

Visit *www.facthound.com*

Just type in **9781543504958** and go.

Check out projects, games and lots more at
www.capstonekids.com

Index